SLAVERY AND RESISTANCE

DRAMA OF AFRICAN-AMERICAN HISTORY

SLAVERY AND RESISTANCE

by ANNE DEVEREAUX JORDAN

with VIRGINIA SCHOMP

Marshall Cavendish
Benchmark
New York

For Kaitlyn, Madelyn, and Luke

With thanks to Jill Watts, professor of history at California State University, San Marcos,
for her perceptive comments on the manuscript, and to the late Richard Newman,
civil rights advocate, author, and senior research officer at the W.E.B. DuBois Institute
at Harvard University, for his excellent work in formulating the series.
With thanks, too, to Kathy Benson and the late James Haskins for their support and friendship.
And, of course, thanks to my son, David.

EDITOR: JOYCE STANTON   EDITORIAL DIRECTOR: MICHELLE BISSON
ART DIRECTOR: ANAHID HAMPARIAN   SERIES DESIGNER: MICHAEL NELSON

MARSHALL CAVENDISH BENCHMARK   99 WHITE PLAINS ROAD   TARRYTOWN, NEW YORK 10591-9001
www.marshallcavendish.us   Text copyright © 2007 by Anne Devereaux Jordan   All rights reserved. No part of this book may be reproduced or utilized in any form or by any means electronic or mechanical including photocopying, recording, or by any information storage and retrieval system, without permission from the copyright holders. All Internet sites were available and accurate when this book was sent to press. LIBRARY OF CONGRESS CATALOGING-IN-PUBLICATION DATA: Jordan, Anne Devereaux. Slavery and resistance / by Anne Devereaux Jordan ; with Virginia Schomp. p. cm. — (Drama of African-American history) Summary: "Describes slavery in the United States from colonial times up to the Civil War"—Provided by publisher. Includes bibliographical references and index. ISBN-13: 978-0-7614-2178-8 ISBN-10: 0-7614-2178-5 1. Slavery—United States—History—Juvenile literature. 2. Antislavery movements—United States—History—Juvenile literature. 3. Slaves—United States—Social conditions—Juvenile literature. 4. Slave insurrections—United States—History—Juvenile literature. 5. African Americans—History—Juvenile literature. I. Schomp, Virginia. II. Title. III. Series. E441.J67 2007 306.3'620973—dc22 2006012313

Images provided by Rose Corbett Gordon, Art Editor, Mystic, CT, from the following sources: Cover: Francis G. Mayer/Corbis Back cover: Brooklyn Museum of Art/ Bridgeman Art Library Page i: Louie Psihoyos/Corbis; pages ii - iii, 26, 30, 44: The Art Archive/Culver Pictures; pages vi, 38: North Wind Picture Archives; page vii: Historical Picture Archive/Corbis; pages viii, 3, 16 top, 16 bottom, 18, 32, 65: The Granger Collection, New York; pages x, 50: SuperStock; pages 4, 12, 14: Bettmann/Corbis; page 6: Private Collection/Bridgeman Art Library; page 8: Private Collection/Art Resource, NY; page 10: Christie's Images/Corbis; page 17: National Portrait Gallery, Smithsonian Institution/Art Resource, NY; page 19: Réunion des Musées Nationaux/Art Resource, NY; page 21: The New Bedford Whaling Museum; page 22: Corbis; page 24: ARPL/HIP/The Image Works; page 34: Atwater Kent Museum of Philadelphia/Courtesy of Historical Society of Pennsylvania Collection/Bridgeman Art Library; page 36: Hulton Archive/Getty Images; page 40: The J. Paul Getty Museum, Los Angeles; pages 41, 58: Library of Congress; pages 46, 48: Snark/Art Resource, NY; page 52: Courtesy of The North Carolina State Archives; page 53: Beinecke Rare Book and Manuscript Library, Yale University; page 56: Art Resource, NY; page 63: New-York Historical Society/Bridgeman Art Library

Printed in China
1 3 5 6 4 2

Front cover: Women and children waiting to be sold at a slave market in Richmond, Virginia, in 1853
Back cover: *A Ride for Liberty, or The Fugitive Slaves*, painted by noted American artist Eastman Johnson in 1862
Title page: Slaves making their way north to freedom hide in a swamp.
p. vi: African captives on board a slave ship off the coast of Florida

CONTENTS

Introduction   vii

Chapter 1
SLAVERY IN COLONIAL AMERICA
1

Chapter 2
REVOLUTION!
13

Chapter 3
"TWO PEOPLES"
25

Chapter 4
PLANTATION LIFE
37

Chapter 5
QUIET RESISTANCE
47

Chapter 6
OPEN REBELLION
59

Glossary   67
To Find Out More   68
Selected Bibliography   68
Index   69

INTRODUCTION

Slavery and Resistance is the third book in the series Drama of African-American History. The first two books in this series looked at Africa, where the story of African Americans began, and at the transatlantic slave trade, which took captive Africans across the Atlantic Ocean to the Americas. In this book we will trace the development of slavery in what is now the United States. We will learn how African Americans struggled against brutality and injustice in a nation founded on principles of liberty, justice, and equality.

Between the mid-1400s and late 1800s, an estimated 30 million to 60 million African men, women, and children were torn from their homes by the transatlantic slave trade. Slave traders came to the west coast of Africa from Portugal, Spain, France, the Netherlands, Britain, and other European countries, as well as from North America. They seized captives or bought them from African slave traders. They loaded the captives into the filthy, crowded cargo holds of slave ships. Then they transported their human cargo across the Atlantic to European colonies in the New World. About one-third of the captive

Africans survived the transatlantic crossing. Most of these were taken to the Caribbean islands (also known as the West Indies) or South America. About half a million ended up in North America, in the British or Spanish colonies that would become the United States.

Britain's first permanent settlement in North America had been established at Jamestown, Virginia, in May 1607. The founders of Jamestown included a large proportion of "gentlemen-adventurers" who were unprepared for the hardships of life in their new wilderness home. Instead of planting crops, they built a wooden fort enclosing houses, a storehouse, and a church. Instead of seeking alliances with the area's Native Americans, they treated their new neighbors with contempt. The colonists

Slaves (and a white overseer) at work on a cotton plantation in the Caribbean

quickly ran through their food supplies. Four months after the Jamestown landing, George Percy wrote that many of his fellow settlers had been

> destroyed with cruell diseases, as Swellings, Flixes [flux, or diarrhea], Burning Fevers, and by warres [wars with the Indians], and some departed suddenly, but for the most part they died of meere famine. There were never Englishmen left in a forreigne Countrey in such miserie as wee were in this new discovered Virginia.

In early 1609 several hundred more Englishmen reached the desperately struggling colony. That winter, in what became known as the "starving time," the people of Jamestown ate through their livestock and began eating pets, mice, rats, and even the bodies of the dead to survive. By spring, only sixty settlers were still alive. Just as the ragged survivors prepared to abandon the colony, three ships arrived from England, bearing a new group of colonists and lifesaving supplies.

The spring also brought a discovery that would mean not only survival but prosperity. The Jamestown colonists found that a prized variety of tobacco flourished in Virginia's fertile soil and warm climate. Before long, tobacco plantations had sprung up all over the region, and planters were raking in huge profits from exports of the valuable crop. In 1619 the thriving colony welcomed its first large group of female settlers, ninety women transported from England at the cost of 120 pounds of tobacco each. That year also brought the colony's first black residents. The British settlers in Jamestown traded their excess food supplies for a Dutch slave ship's cargo of twenty captive Africans.

Tabacum latifolium.

A drawing of the leaves and flowers of the profitable tobacco plant

The British had little experience with slavery. In fact, they looked down on the Spanish and Portuguese, who dominated the transatlantic slave trade and used slave labor on their New World plantations. In place of this "foreign" practice, the British intended to rely on indentured servants as the main

SLAVERY AND RESISTANCE

source of labor in their American colonies. These working-class men and women contracted to serve a master for a set number of years in exchange for food, clothing, shelter, and the cost of transportation from England. At the end of their term of service, which usually lasted from five to seven years, indentured servants were entitled to their freedom.

The first Africans in Jamestown were treated more like indentured servants than slaves. They worked alongside white servants in the shops and tobacco fields. They had the same legal rights, including the right to marry, sue in the courts, and accumulate property. Although they had to serve their masters longer than white servants did, sometimes as long as twenty years, they were free when their term of indenture ended.

Over time, the white settlers of colonial America would begin to make greater distinctions between white and black servants. While whites continued to earn their freedom, new laws would place increasing restrictions on black rights and liberties. Blacks would gradually become the main source of labor in the growing American colonies, and race would become the sole factor determining who was free and who was enslaved for life.

"Sold to the highest bidder!" the auctioneer might be saying. In colonial America, the institution of slavery grew stronger and harsher after the mid-1600s, when slaves were declared to be "real estate."

Chapter 1

SLAVERY IN COLONIAL AMERICA

In 1621 an African listed as "Antonio, a Negro" was sold to Edward Bennett, a tobacco planter in Jamestown. Antonio married Mary, another African servant on the Bennett plantation. The couple worked for fourteen years to buy their way out of servitude. By the early 1640s, they were both free settlers, making the most of the opportunities open to hardworking, ambitious people in the New World. Antonio took the name Anthony Johnson. He moved with Mary and their four children to the eastern shore of Virginia. There the family settled on a small farm, growing tobacco and raising livestock. In time they acquired 250 acres of land and several servants, black and white. When a fire destroyed their plantation in 1653, they appealed to the county for help to rebuild. A court agreed to reduce the

Johnsons' taxes, noting that the couple had been "inhabitants in Virginia above thirty yeares" and praising their "hard labor and known service."

THE TERRIBLE TRANSFORMATION

Anthony and Mary Johnson belonged to the first generation of African Americans. When they settled on Virginia's eastern shore in the mid-1600s, there were only a few thousand Africans in North America. Most of these black residents had arrived on slave ships from the Caribbean Islands.

White indentured servants far outnumbered Africans in early colonial America. Colonial laws made few distinctions between the two groups. Like whites, Africans could marry, raise families, travel throughout the mainland, sue in the courts, and own property. Although blacks had to serve longer terms of indenture than white servants, they eventually might earn their freedom. About one-fifth of the African Americans on the eastern shore of Virginia, where Anthony Johnson lived, were free.

Life was harder for the children and grandchildren of the first African Americans. Through a gradual process that some historians have called the "terrible transformation," the institution of race slavery grew stronger and harsher after the mid-1600s. That change took place in different ways throughout the emerging colonies.

THE CHESAPEAKE COLONIES

The terrible transformation began in the area around Chesapeake Bay, an inlet of the Atlantic Ocean bordered by Virginia and Maryland. The British established the Maryland colony

Jamestown colonists load their tobacco crop onto English ships.

about twenty-five years after the founding of Jamestown. Like their neighbors in Virginia, many of Maryland's settlers planted tobacco. The tobacco plantations of the Chesapeake region were fairly small, averaging about 250 acres. The labor on these plantations was performed mainly by white indentured servants, along with some black slaves.

Around the mid-1600s Chesapeake planters began to feel the pinch of a labor shortage. For a number of reasons, including a declining population and increased job opportunities in England, fewer white servants were migrating to the colonies. To fill out their workforce, planters began to buy more African laborers. Slave traders responded to the rising demand by importing more and more captives not only from the Caribbean but also directly from Africa.

As Africans became an increasingly important source of labor in the Chesapeake region, planters recognized the advantages that permanent black enslavement offered them. White indentured servants who ran away before fulfilling their contracts could escape capture by blending into the population. Those who worked long enough to earn their freedom could become planters themselves, competing for land and labor. Basing slavery on skin color solved these problems. It was easy to identify a black slave. Also, while it cost more to buy a slave than to import an indentured servant, slaves could be held for life. And the fact that their children could also become the slaveholder's property made Africans an even more attractive investment.

To protect slaveholders' investments and control the black population, colonial leaders passed a series of laws known as the slave codes. These laws gradually nibbled away at the rights and opportunities of African Americans. Virginia recognized slavery as a legal institution in 1661, Maryland in 1664. Other slave codes declared that slaves were "real estate" and that their children belonged to their white masters. Under a law passed in Virginia in 1705, a master who committed murder while "correcting" a disobedient slave would be "free of all punishment . . . as if such accident never happened." A 1740

A slave is tied to a water pump and doused repeatedly as punishment for disobedience.

law permitted the execution of a slave who conspired to run away, burned a "stack of rice," or taught another slave "the knowledge of any poisonous root, plant [or] herb."

In 1665, following a dispute with a white neighbor, Anthony Johnson moved to Maryland. The Johnson family settled on a three-hundred-acre farm, which they called Tonies Vineyard. Two years later, a white planter stole a large shipment of tobacco belonging to the Johnsons. The planter produced a forged letter, supposedly written and signed by Anthony, which "proved" that the African owed him an amount of money equal to the value of the tobacco. Despite the fact that Anthony Johnson could not read or write, a court upheld the white man's claim.

THE LOWER SOUTH

While the Chesapeake region shifted to permanent black slavery gradually, other parts of the South embraced the institution almost immediately. Most of the early settlers of the Carolina colony (present-day North Carolina and South Carolina) came from Barbados, a British colony in the West Indies where thousands of African slaves labored on sugar plantations. The Africans who came to Carolina with the first white settlers were already enslaved. In 1669 the colony's constitution declared that "every freeman of Carolina, shall have absolute power and authority over his negro slaves."

The main export of the "low country" region that would become South Carolina was rice. Tens of thousands of African slaves were imported to work on the vast rice plantations, which often sprawled over a thousand acres or more. By 1750,

The South's vast rice plantations needed a great many slaves to keep them in business.

blacks outnumbered whites by more than six to one in South Carolina. To control its large black population, the colony passed increasingly strict slave codes. One law passed in 1740 forbade slaves to buy or sell goods, raise livestock, own boats or canoes, carry arms, gather or travel in groups, or learn to read and write.

Georgia was the last of Britain's North American colonies to legalize slavery. The settlers who founded the southern colony in 1733 called it "shocking to human nature that any race of Mankind and their Posterity [descendants], should be sentenced to perpetual Slavery." Within two decades, however, the Georgia legislature had bowed to the demands of plantation owners and legalized slavery. Slave traders quickly imported a flood of African slaves to work on the colony's huge rice and indigo plantations. By 1770, blacks made up more than 45 percent of Georgia's population.

Florida was settled by Spain in the mid-1500s. Both free and enslaved Africans arrived with the first Spanish settlers in the Florida colony. Under Spanish rule, African slaves had more rights than those in the British colonies, including the right to work independently and earn their freedom. In 1763, however, Britain won control of Florida, and slaves lost most of their

AN UNCERTAIN FREEDOM

In 1770 there were an estimated 40,000 free blacks in colonial America. These included former indentured servants, descendants of indentured servants, slaves who had escaped their masters, and black immigrants from the Caribbean Islands. The slave codes did not apply to free blacks. However, even in the northern colonies, where slavery was generally less brutal than in the South, free African Americans struggled against racist laws and policies.

In some parts of both the North and South, free blacks were not allowed to own land or livestock. They could not travel without a pass or settle in a town without special permission. Although they might be taxed, they could not vote. No matter how hardworking or skilled they might be, many banks denied them credit and many employers refused to hire them.

Some laws were targeted specifically at free blacks. Under a Virginia statute, any black person who gained his or her freedom had to leave the colony within six months. In Pennsylvania free blacks could be ordered back into servitude for crimes such as aiding a runaway slave, marrying a white person, or "laziness." In New York blacks who could not show proof of their freedom could be arrested on suspicion of being runaways. These suspects were held in jail while the authorities advertised in the newspapers, seeking their owners. The detainees might be released to any white person who claimed them. If they went unclaimed, the authorities sometimes sold them into slavery to recover the costs of imprisoning and advertising them.

rights and privileges. Rice and indigo plantations sprang up throughout the colony, and the number of slaves imported from Africa increased dramatically. By 1770, a visitor touring Florida observed that on many Florida estates, it was impossible to find a single "white face belonging to the plantation save [except] an overseer."

New England and the Middle Colonies

There were no large plantations in New England (Massachusetts, New Hampshire, Connecticut, Rhode Island) or the Middle Colonies (New York, New Jersey, Pennsylvania, Delaware). Instead, settlers worked on small farms and practiced a wide variety of trades. As a result, the experiences of slaves in the northern colonies was very different from those in the South.

The first white settlement in New England was founded by the Pilgrims at Plymouth, Massachusetts, in 1620. Ten years later, another group of British colonists arrived in Boston and founded the Massachusetts Bay Colony. Many of these settlers were Puritans, members of a strict Protestant group who hoped to create a "city upon a hill" where they could live according to their religious beliefs. While the Puritans were intensely spiritual, they were also very practical. They needed cheap labor to establish their new colony, and it was far less expensive to buy slaves than to maintain indentured servants. Emanuel Downing, who settled in Massachusetts in 1638, wrote to relatives back in England that the colony would never thrive "until we gett . . . a stock of slaves sufficient to doe all our business."

In 1641 Massachusetts became the first British colony in North America to declare slavery a legal institution. Within a few years, Connecticut, Rhode Island, and New Hampshire had also legalized human bondage. In addition, New England became increasingly active in the transatlantic slave trade. Ships owned by merchants in Massachusetts and neighboring colonies transported thousands of captive Africans to the southern colonies and the Caribbean.

The first white settlements in the Middle Colonies were established by the Dutch West India Company, which dominated the transatlantic slave trade in the mid-1600s. In 1624 the Dutch company founded the colony of New Netherland along the Hudson River. Eager to expand the market for African slaves, company officials pledged to "use their endeavors to supply the colonists with as many Blacks as they conveniently can." Hundreds of slaves were transported to New Netherland

A typical small farm in one of the Middle Colonies. Although these farms did not require great numbers of laborers, their white owners still believed that it was economically sound to own black slaves.

to clear the land, build roads, and construct homes and public buildings. The Dutch West India Company also carried slaves to its outlying settlements in the Delaware Valley.

In 1664 Britain captured New Netherland from the Dutch and divided the colony into New York and New Jersey. The British also seized control of Dutch possessions in the Delaware Valley, which would become the colonies of Pennsylvania and Delaware. Under British rule, New York joined the transatlantic slave trade, importing thousands of slaves from Africa and the West Indies. Soon the colony had the largest slave population north of Maryland.

Despite New York's relatively large slave population, the number of African Americans in the North never came close to that in the southern colonies. Nevertheless, slaves played an important role in the North's diverse economy. Enslaved Africans worked on small farms in New England and the Middle Colonies. They managed their owners' shops and businesses, acted as cooks and personal servants, and worked in trades such as lumbering, blacksmithing, carpentry, brewing, and printing. Slaves also made up a large portion of the workforce in industries such as shipbuilding and sailmaking in Rhode Island and Massachusetts, ironworking in Pennsylvania, and the tanning of animal hides in New York.

In this sentimental painting, a devoted slave offers a bowl of soup to her elderly master.

Because there were fewer blacks in the North than in the South, northern legislators did not feel the need to pass as many laws to control them. In some parts of the North, both free blacks and slaves could own and inherit property. Blacks also had some of the same rights as whites in court. On the other hand, some states passed slave codes restricting the rights of slaves and free blacks to assemble and travel. In New York each county had a "Negro Whipper," whose job was to flog any black person who violated a law prohibiting more than three blacks from meeting without their owners' permission. Most importantly, slaves were considered property. They could be bought and sold at the whim of their owners. Many northern black families were broken apart when husbands were sold away from wives, sisters from brothers, parents from children.

In the spring of 1670, Anthony Johnson died a free man. After his death his wife, Mary, and their oldest son, Richard, became owners of the family's estate in Virginia. A few months later, however, an all-white jury ruled that the land had never really belonged to Anthony, because he "was a Negroe and by consequence an alien" without property rights. The court seized the estate and divided it between two neighboring white planters. Some time later, Richard Johnson and his brother, John, bought a small farm in Maryland, which they named Angola after their father's African birthplace. The records of the Johnson family end with the deaths of Anthony Johnson's grandchildren, the third generation of African Americans to struggle against the overwhelming tide of American slavery.

Patriot leader Patrick Henry delivers the famous speech in which he proclaimed, "Give me liberty, or give me death!"

Chapter 2

REVOLUTION!

THE ROOTS OF THE AMERICAN REVOLUTION WERE planted in the French and Indian War. From 1754 to 1763, the British fought the French and their Native American allies for control of territories in North America. Britain won the war, but the long struggle left the nation deeply in debt. The British decided to raise money through taxes in their American colonies. Colonists objected, arguing that Britain had no right to tax them, because they had no representatives in the British Parliament. Following fierce and sometimes violent colonial resistance, Britain sent hundreds of red-coated soldiers to Boston to restore order. The British also punished the colonies with a series of tough new measures that Americans called the Intolerable Acts.

In 1774 the First Continental Congress met in Philadelphia to work out the American response to Britain's actions. The delegates declared the right of Americans to pass their own laws and taxes. They urged citizens to begin arming themselves for a military showdown. "War is inevitable," cried Patriot leader Patrick Henry of Virginia. "I know not what course others may take; but as for me, give me liberty, or give me death!"

"Liberty! Liberty!"

On the eve of the Revolutionary War, one out of every five Americans was black. More than 90 percent of black Americans—about half a million men, women, and children—were slaves. The hearts of these oppressed people lifted as they heard the Patriots' cries for liberty. Surely a struggle for independence and political freedom held the promise of personal freedom, too.

That might have been the thinking of the first American to die in the early days of the conflict with the British. His name was Crispus Attucks, and he was a runaway slave. Following a

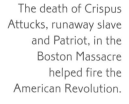

The death of Crispus Attucks, runaway slave and Patriot, in the Boston Massacre helped fire the American Revolution.

confrontation between civilians and Redcoats on the streets of Boston in March 1770, Attucks had led a mob of about thirty men and boys to the Customs House. The mob threw rocks and icy snowballs at the British guards. The soldiers opened fire. According to published accounts, Attucks was "killed on the Spot, two [musket] balls entering his Breast." Four other Americans also died. As news of the "Boston Massacre" spread through the colonies, the former slave became a hero of the Patriot cause.

Many other African Americans took part in the events leading up to the Revolution. Both free and enslaved blacks joined the crowds shouting "No taxation without representation" all across the colonies. They paraded with white Patriots in New York, Boston, Philadelphia, and other towns. However, black participation in these demonstrations made many white colonists uneasy, especially in the South. In Charleston, South Carolina, white residents became alarmed by the growing number of slaves echoing Patriot cries of "Liberty! Liberty!" Afraid that the black demonstrators might be encouraged to strike out for their own freedom, authorities called out armed guards to silence them.

CONFLICTS AND CONTRADICTIONS

While black Americans joined the colonial protests against British repression, they also reminded their white countrymen of the contradictions in their calls for liberty. How could Patriots support black slavery while proclaiming that Americans would never be England's "slaves"? A petition sent by four black slaves to the Massachusetts legislature opened with these comments:

The efforts made by the legislative of this province in their last sessions to free themselves from slavery gave us, who are in that deplorable state, a high degree of satisfaction. We expect great things from men who have made such a noble stand against the designs of their fellow-men to enslave them. We cannot but wish and hope Sir, that you will have the same grand object, we mean civil and religious liberty, in view in your next session.

James Armistead Lafayette served the American forces so well as a spy during the Revolution that the Virginia legislature bought him his freedom.

Some white Americans agreed that it was hypocritical to demand freedom for themselves while denying it to the slaves. "To contend for liberty," wrote Patriot leader John Jay, "and to deny that blessing to others involves an inconsistency not to be excused." Abigail Adams reminded her husband, future president John Adams, that white colonists were preparing "to fight ourselves for what we are daily robbing and plundering from those who have as good a right to freedom as we have." The British were only too happy to agree. "How is it that we hear the loudest *yelps* for liberty among the drivers of negroes?" asked British writer Samuel Johnson.

Abigail Adams spoke up for the rights of slaves and women during the Revolutionary War.

A few white colonists responded to these contradictions by calling for the abolition of slavery. Among the first abolitionists were the Quakers, members of a Christian community living mainly in Pennsylvania. In 1775 the Quakers founded the Pennsylvania Society for the Abolition of Slavery, the first abolitionist group in America. During the Revolution, a number of other white Americans would join the small but growing abolition movement. However, the institution of slavery was woven deep into the fabric of colonial society, and it would not easily be destroyed.

The Declaration of Independence

On April 19, 1775, British troops searching for a weapons stockpile in Lexington, Massachusetts, exchanged fire with colonial militiamen. The Redcoats continued on to Concord, where colonists firing from behind stone walls and trees halted their advance. The Revolutionary War had begun.

Quaker preacher and abolitionist Benjamin Lay refused to wear, eat, or use anything produced by slave labor.

Two months after the Battles of Lexington and Concord, the bloodiest battle of the Revolution was fought in Boston. More than one thousand Redcoats and four hundred Americans died in the Battle of Breed's Hill (traditionally known as Bunker Hill). The British won, retaining their hold on Boston, but the Americans showed that they could hold their own against the Redcoats. Among the American casualties was Peter Salem, a former slave. According to eyewitness accounts, Salem was killed after fatally wounding Major John Pitcairn, the leader of the British forces storming American positions on the hill.

More battles followed, with victories and losses on both sides. Over time the colonists abandoned all hopes of restoring former relations with their "mother country." In June 1776 the delegates meeting at the Second Continental Congress in

Philadelphia voted to sever America's ties with Great Britain. Thomas Jefferson, a young Virginia lawyer known for his "happy talent of composition," was assigned the job of drafting the Declaration of Independence. The stirring words of the Declaration had special significance for African Americans:

> We hold these Truths to be self-evident, that all Men are created equal, that they are endowed by their Creator with certain unalienable Rights, that among these are Life, Liberty, and the pursuit of Happiness.

Events in the coming months and years, however, would make it clear that liberty was meant for whites only.

Peter Salem with Lieutenant Thomas Grosvenor at the Battle of Bunker Hill. Salem was a freed slave who had already fought as a Minuteman in the Battle of Concord.

CHOOSING SIDES

African-American militiamen fought the British at Lexington and Concord. More than a hundred black volunteers, including Peter Salem, fought at Bunker Hill. However, many southern slaveholders worried that arming blacks would lead to a slave rebellion. Bowing to these concerns, the Second Continental Congress agreed to exclude slaves and free blacks from the national army organized in the summer of 1775. On November 12, George Washington, the commander of the new Continental army, issued an order forbidding the enlistment of "Negroes, Boys unable to bear Arms [and] Old Men unfit to endure the Fatigues of the Campaign."

THOMAS JEFFERSON, SLAVEHOLDER

One-third of the signers of the Declaration of Independence owned slaves. That included Thomas Jefferson, the document's primary author. Although Jefferson was a lifelong slaveholder, he became increasingly uncomfortable with the institution. His original draft of the Declaration included a paragraph condemning King George III of England for carrying on the transatlantic slave trade, which Jefferson called a "cruel war against human nature itself." After a number of delegates to the Second Continental Congress objected to the antislavery statement, it was stricken from the final version.

In the years following the Revolution, Thomas Jefferson made it clear that he loathed slavery. As governor of Virginia, U.S. congressman, and third president of the United States, he repeatedly wrote about his opposition to this "great political and moral evil." Yet Jefferson also made it clear that he considered people of African heritage less intelligent than whites and better suited for hard labor. When he died in 1826, he still owned about two hundred slaves. Some historians have criticized him for not doing more for the antislavery cause. Others have pointed out that, by introducing the ideals of liberty, equality, and natural rights into the Declaration of Independence, Jefferson set off a chain of events that would in time lead America to abolition.

Above: Monticello, Thomas Jefferson's Virginia estate, was worked by slaves.

Two days later, John Murray, Earl of Dunmore and royal governor of Virginia, countered with a proclamation promising freedom to any slave who would fight for the British. Word of the proclamation spread quickly through the colonies, and thousands of slaves fled their masters. By the war's end, about one thousand fugitive slaves had fought in Lord Dunmore's Ethiopian Regiment, and many more had served the British army as laborers, servants, cooks, guides, and spies.

Meanwhile, American opposition to black enlistment soon faded in the face of Britain's larger and better-equipped forces. In late 1777, 11,000 Continental soldiers settled into the army's winter camp at Valley Forge, Pennsylvania. By the following spring, about 2,500 had died from cold, hunger, or disease. Desperate for new recruits, regiments in the northern colonies began to enlist free blacks as well as slaves, who were promised freedom in return for faithful service. Eventually every colony except Georgia, North Carolina, and South Carolina accepted blacks into its military ranks. Most black soldiers served side by side with whites in integrated units. "No Regiment is to be seen," observed one officer, "in which there are not Negroes in abundance; and among these are able-bodied, strong, and brave fellows."

About 5,000 of the estimated 200,000 men who served in the colonial militias or the Continental army during the Revolutionary War were black. African Americans also served in the Continental navy and aboard privateers, privately owned ships that attacked and plundered enemy vessels. In addition, many black women served the army as cooks, nurses, and laborers.

CONSTITUTIONAL COMPROMISES

In October 1781 British forces surrendered to George Washington at Yorktown, Virginia. Two years later, Great Britain and the United States signed the Treaty of Paris, which formally ended the war and recognized U.S. independence.

More than 14,000 fugitive slaves left the new nation with the withdrawing British troops. A number of other blacks who had sided with the British fled to Canada. The American victory also brought freedom to thousands of slaves who had fought with the Continental forces. However, the end of the American Revolution did not mean the end of slavery in the United States.

During the Revolution, many northerners had become convinced that slavery had no place in a nation founded on ideals of

New Bedford, Massachusetts, in 1810. By this time, slavery played almost no role in the North's economy.

liberty and equality. Beginning in 1777, all of the northern states drafted constitutions that called for immediate or gradual abolition. In most of the South, however, the institution of slavery not only survived but grew stronger than ever.

The war had devastated the American economy. In order for the South to recover, plantations had to quickly become productive again. Southerners called for the resumption of the transatlantic slave trade, which had been halted during wartime, so that they could rebuild their plantation workforces. They also made it clear that they would never accept a federal government that limited their right to hold property, including human property.

After the Revolution, slavery became more important than ever in the South, especially on cotton plantations.

SLAVERY AND RESISTANCE

In 1787 the Constitutional Convention met in Philadelphia. Eager to avoid conflicts that might threaten the unity of the new nation, northern delegates agreed to allow the slave trade to continue for twenty years. They also gave in to southern demands for a constitutional provision prohibiting any state from passing laws that would free a "person held to service or labor" in another state. In their most heated debates, northern and southern delegates considered the question of whether slaves should be counted as part of a state's population. Northerners did not want to count slaves, because that would give the southern states greater representation in Congress. Southerners feared that the northern states would gain too much political power if slaves were not counted. In the end the delegates decided that, in determining the population of a state, each slave resident would count as three-fifths of a person.

The Constitution of the United States, ratified in 1788, did not include the words *slavery* or *slave*. By protecting slave property and increasing the political influence of slaveholders, however, the Constitution threw the power of the federal government behind the institution of slavery. "No mention was made of negroes or slaves in this constitution," wrote Patriot leader Benjamin Rush, "only because it was thought the very words would contaminate the glorious fabric of American liberty and government. Thus you see the cloud, which a few years ago was no larger than a man's hand, . . . at last covered every part of our land."

A slave auction shop in Atlanta, Georgia, around 1860. While slavery died out in the North after the Revolutionary War, it flourished in the South.

Chapter 3

"Two Peoples"

MANY OF AMERICA'S FOUNDING FATHERS REGARDED slavery as primitive and immoral. Despite the compromises between pro- and antislavery forces at the Constitutional Convention, these leaders hoped that the institution would die a "natural death" in the new nation. George Washington wrote that it was one of his greatest wishes that "slavery in this Country may be abolished by slow, sure and imperceptible degrees."

Despite such wishes, slavery would not die away in the years following the American Revolution. Instead, while the movement toward abolition took hold in the North, slavery would flourish in the South and spread westward with the growing nation. To one northern newspaper editor, it would soon seem that Americans had become "two peoples. We are a people for Freedom and a people for slavery. Between the two, conflict is inevitable."

THE COTTON KINGDOM

According to the 1790 census, more than 650,000 of the nearly 698,000 slaves in the United States lived in the South. By 1830, the North held only about 3,500 slaves, while the South had more than 2 million. Thirty years later, there would be nearly 4 million slaves in the South, more than in the rest of the world combined.

The main reason for the rapid expansion of southern slavery was cotton. In pre-Revolutionary times most slaves had labored on plantations growing tobacco, rice, or indigo. Cotton cultivation was limited, because it was very time-consuming to separate the seeds from the harvested crop. Then, in 1793, Eli

Bales of cotton crowd the docks in Charleston, South Carolina. The cotton will be loaded onto ships and taken to factories in the North or overseas.

Whitney invented an engine, or "gin," for cleaning cotton. A worker operating a cotton gin could clean fifty times as much cotton in a day as a laborer picking out the seeds by hand. That made cotton growing far more efficient and profitable.

In 1795, the first year of the cotton gin's operation, American planters produced 8 million pounds of cotton. By 1800, production had increased more than 400 percent, and it would continue to double every decade until the Civil War. Nearly all of the South's raw cotton was exported to factories in New England and Britain, where steam-driven machines spun it into yarn and wove the yarn into fabric. Cotton quickly became the United States' leading export, bringing in more revenue than all other exports combined.

The cotton boom not only revitalized the southern economy but also brought new life to the institution of slavery. More and more laborers were needed for the backbreaking task of planting and harvesting the cotton crop. To meet that demand, increasing numbers of slaves were transported from Africa and from northern states to the South. For many Africans and Americans of African descent, the invention of the cotton gin meant not progress but decades of misery.

SLAVERY MOVES WEST

Before the Revolution, slavery was restricted to a string of colonies along America's east coast. By the beginning of the Civil War in 1861, it had spread halfway across the continent. The spread of slavery to the Southwest was spurred mainly by cotton production.

In 1803 President Thomas Jefferson purchased the Louisiana Territory from France. The Louisiana Purchase doubled

The plantations of the Cotton Kingdom were worked almost entirely by slaves.

the size of the nation, extending U.S. borders westward from the Mississippi River to the Rocky Mountains and north from the Gulf of Mexico to Canada. The southern part of the new territory had rich soil, a warm climate, and abundant rainfall. Those conditions were ideal for growing cotton. Many planters in the coastal states quickly rounded up their slaves and moved west. Soon vast fields of cotton were growing in a long belt that stretched from South Carolina all the way to the Mexican territory of Texas. Over the next few decades, slave traders would transport thousands of slaves to the new cotton-growing region. Cotton was still the main crop in the southern coastal states, especially South Carolina, Georgia, and Florida. However, the new states of Alabama, Mississippi, and Louisiana would become the heart of the Cotton Kingdom.

THE DOMESTIC SLAVE TRADE

Following the end of the Revolutionary War, thousands of captive Africans were transported into slavery in the United States. Then the constitutional provision allowing the transatlantic slave trade to continue for twenty years expired. In January 1808 President Thomas Jefferson signed the Act to Prohibit the Importation of Slaves.

Abolitionists hoped that slavery would die out with the official termination of the transatlantic slave trade. Their hopes were soon disappointed. Smugglers continued to import a steady stream of African captives right up to the Civil War. Even more significantly, the end of legal international slave trading and the rise of the Cotton Kingdom led to a vast expansion of the domestic slave trade.

Since colonial times slaveholders had bought and sold their human property. Now the intense demand for laborers to work in southern cotton fields increased the value of slaves both in states that raised cotton and those that did not. Slaveholders in non-cotton-producing states found that they could make a handsome profit selling their "surplus" slaves to the cotton planters. Between 1790 and 1860, an estimated one million slaves were sold in the upper South, mainly in Virginia, Maryland, Delaware, and North Carolina. Most of these captives were taken to states in the lower South and Southwest, including Georgia, South Carolina, Alabama, Mississippi, Louisiana, and Texas.

While some slaves were sold privately, from one planter to another, most were bought and sold by professional slave traders. Domestic slave traders bought black men, women, and children from individual owners and shipped them to market by boat, railroad, or in slave coffles. A slave coffle was a long line of shackled captives who were bound together by ropes or chains. Coffles often marched for twenty-five or thirty miles a day under a slave driver's whip. After days or weeks of hard travel, they reached slave markets in the countryside or in large

Shackled and bound together by chains, slaves in a coffle pass through Washington, DC, in 1815.

cities such as Natchez, Mississippi; Montgomery, Alabama; and New Orleans, Louisiana. Anne Maddox, who was shipped from Virginia to Alabama at age thirteen, later recalled the horrors of a slave market crowded with "white peoples . . . from everywhere; the face of the earth was covered by them."

For slaves, being "sold south" usually meant permanent separation from home, friends, and family. Charles Ball was four years old when his family was split up after the death of their master in Maryland.

My new master . . . took me before him on his horse, and started home, but my poor mother, when she saw me leaving her for the last time, ran after me. . . . The slave-driver . . . gave her two or three heavy blows on the shoulders with his rawhide, snatched me from her arms, handed me to my master, and seizing her by one arm, dragged her back towards the place of sale. My master then quickened the pace of his horse; and as we advanced, the cries of my poor parent became more and more indistinct—at length they died away in the distance, and I never again heard the voice of my poor mother.

Years later, Charles Ball was sold to a cotton planter in South Carolina. He marched south with fifty-one other slaves fitted with iron collars and "handcuffed in pairs, with iron staples and bolts." Ball left behind a wife and several children in Maryland. He managed to escape and return home, only to find that "some slave-dealer had come in my absence and seized my wife and children as slaves, and sold them to such men as I had served in the South. They had now passed into hopeless bondage, and were gone forever."

FREEDOM IN THE SOUTH

Alongside the slaves in the southern states lived thousands of free African Americans. Most free southern blacks lived in the upper South, in states including Delaware, Maryland, and Virginia. In 1810 there were about 94,000 free blacks in the upper South, making up more than 10 percent of the region's total black population. Meanwhile, in the lower or "deep" South, only about 14,000 African Americans, or less than 4 percent of the black population, were free. The living conditions of free blacks were quite different in the two regions.

Most free blacks in the lower South were "mulattoes," or light-skinned descendants of African slaves and white colonists. The mulattoes were usually treated with grudging acceptance by their white neighbors. Many held lower-level jobs as servants, laborers, or peddlers, but a significant minority worked at skilled occupations such as carpentry or barbering. A few mulattoes managed to accumulate considerable wealth and property. For most, however, life was a constant struggle against poverty and racism. State and local laws denied them the right to vote and restricted their movements. In Charleston,

South Carolina, free blacks were required to wear a special tag decorated with a liberty cap. In Mississippi they had to carry a certificate of registration proving their free status. Any African American found without an up-to-date tag or certificate could be jailed and sold at a slave auction.

Free African Americans in the upper South were generally darker-skinned than those in the lower South. About two-thirds of the free blacks in the upper South lived in the countryside, where they usually worked as farmhands or common laborers. In cities such as Baltimore and Washington, DC, free blacks might be factory workers, laborers, or servants in white households. Wherever they lived, they faced nearly constant discrimination. Laws in most parts of the upper South banned blacks from voting or joining the militias. Blacks were excluded from schools, theaters, and many other public facilities. Regulations and curfews prevented their traveling and assembling freely, which made it difficult to organize black schools, churches, and social groups.

A free African American proudly poses for his portrait in 1852.

Free blacks throughout the South could not even count on their freedom. In 1793 the southern-dominated Congress passed the Fugitive Slave Act. Under that law, a slaveholder could have any African American arrested on suspicion of being a runaway slave. Even a free black could be seized and taken before the local authorities, who could declare that the accused person was the slaveholder's property.

Northern free states often refused to enforce the law. In

response Congress passed an even harsher measure. Under the Fugitive Slave Act of 1850, all law officers and citizens were required to help capture and return suspected runaways. The law denied captives the right to speak in their own defense. Only slaveholders were permitted to offer testimony "proving" that an accused fugitive should be returned to slavery.

FREEDOM IN THE NORTH

By 1840, nearly all African Americans living in the North were free. Some former slaves had earned their freedom through service in the Revolutionary War. Others had been freed by their masters during or after the Revolution. Still others were set free by the laws and constitutions of the emerging states.

The majority of northern African Americans lived in Philadelphia, New York, Boston, and other large cities. Most worked as seamen, laborers, or domestic servants in white households. A small but growing minority of free blacks worked in trades or professions, often catering mainly to black clients. They might be doctors, teachers, clergymen, musicians, carpenters, tailors, bakers, shoemakers, sailmakers, hairdressers, or shop owners. Together the freedmen in northern cities formed vibrant new black communities. They built black churches, schools, and libraries. They founded literary groups, debating clubs, cultural societies, and mutual aid societies, which provided members with benefits such as insurance and burial.

Outside the cities, most free northern blacks worked as farmers. Black farmers usually labored on small plots of land that they rented from white landowners. A few former slaves worked their way out of poverty to buy and farm their own land.

THE COLONIZATION MOVEMENT

In the early 1800s, the persecution of free African Americans led to the colonization movement. Paul Cuffee, a Quaker sea captain of African-American and Native American descent, was the first to propose resettling free blacks in Africa, where they might enjoy "every privlege of free born Subjects." Cuffee died in 1817, at the very beginning of his venture. However, his efforts inspired Robert Finley, a white clergyman from New Jersey, to found the American Colonization Society. In 1822 the society established a colony on the west coast of Africa, which would later become the independent nation of Liberia. Over time the American Colonization Society transported about 12,000 African-American emigrants to Liberia.

The reaction of African Americans to the colonization movement was mixed. Some supported the idea because they believed that blacks would never receive justice and equality in the United States. Others attacked colonization as a white scheme to rid the country of its free black population. The great majority of African Americans simply rejected the idea of moving to a distant and unknown land. For better or worse, the country where their ancestors had been brought against their will was home.

Above: Edward James Roye, born in Ohio, immigrated to Liberia in 1846 and became its fifth president in 1870.

Like their cousins in the upper South, free northern blacks nearly always faced hardship, discrimination, and hostility. They were barred from most public schools. They were often denied the right to vote, file lawsuits, testify in court, and sit on juries. White employers and workers excluded them from higher-paying occupations. In addition, free blacks were often the target of hatred and violence. They were attacked by whites who objected to working with them or living near them. Black schools were vandalized, and black churches were burned. Like their southern cousins, northern blacks also faced the risk of being kidnapped and forced back into slavery under the fugitive slave laws.

Chapter 4

PLANTATION LIFE

THE LIVING CONDITIONS OF SLAVES IN THE AMERICAN South varied greatly, depending mainly on where they lived. Some slaves labored on large plantations. Others worked alongside their masters on small farms. Slaves might live on isolated farmsteads, cut off from other African Americans, or in more populated communities, where they were able to visit neighboring plantations. A few lived in cities. These urban slaves enjoyed considerably more freedom of movement and association than country slaves. According to the African-American publisher and abolitionist Frederick Douglass, city slaves also suffered less cruelty than slaves on isolated farms and plantations. Only a "desperate slaveholder," wrote Douglass, "will shock the humanity of his non-slaveholding neighbors with the cries of his lacerated slave."

Slaves plant sweet potatoes on a farm on Edisto Island, South Carolina.

Despite the differences in the conditions of their enslavement, there were some things that nearly all African-American slaves had in common. Their lives were controlled by masters who regarded them first and foremost as property. They could be bought, sold, starved, raped, beaten, or worked to death at the whim of their owners. And they were doomed to see their children born into a life of endless indignity, pain, and hardship.

BACKBREAKING LABOR

The great majority of slaves worked on farms or plantations where cotton, sugar, tobacco, rice, and other crops were grown. On a large plantation, there might be about fifty or more slaves. However, most slaves lived on smaller farms, in groups of ten or less.

Some plantation slaves worked in the grand home of the master and his family. Servants in the "big house" cooked, cleaned, waited on table, made and repaired clothing, acted as maids and valets, drove carriages, gardened, and took care of the master's children. Slaves on plantations also might practice skilled crafts such as carpentry, blacksmithing, or shoemaking.

Most plantation slaves worked in the fields. They plowed, planted, weeded, and brought in the harvests.

A young slave serves drinks to a group of men relaxing in the "big house" on a Louisiana plantation.

SLAVERY AND RESISTANCE

Field hands also labored at clearing land, digging ditches, building fences, cutting trees, hauling logs, and many other tasks. Slaves traditionally worked six days a week, with Sundays off. Some masters gave their laborers an additional half day on Saturday, while others worked their slaves seven days a week.

The field hands' workday generally began at sunrise and ended at sunset, with a couple of short breaks for meals. The slaves usually ate their breakfast and lunch in the fields. A common meal was hoecake, made from a mixture of cornmeal, water, and salt, which was heated on a hoe held over an open fire. In the evenings, after their work in the fields was finished, slaves usually had other chores. One might feed the mules, another the pigs, while a third chopped wood or carried water to the big house.

The workday was extended at harvesttime. Slaves might go to work before sunrise and toil far into the night by the light of the moon or lanterns. One Florida planter boasted that he worked his slaves "in a hurrying time till 11 or 12 o'clock at night and [had] them up by four in the morning."

WOMEN AND CHILDREN

Enslaved women generally worked alongside the men in the fields. At night they often helped their mistress with "women's work" such as cooking, cleaning, spinning, and sewing. A slave known as Engineer Ted told Fanny Kemble, the new mistress of a Georgia plantation, that his wife was dying from a lifetime of backbreaking labor. "She had to work in the rice fields," wrote Kemble, "and was 'most broke in two' with labor and exposure and hard work while with child, and hard work just

The children of plantation owners were often cared for by women slaves, who might be separated from their own children at any time.

Portrait of a Nurse and Young Child (detail), c. 1850, unknown maker, American

directly after child-bearing; he said she could hardly crawl, . . . and he thought she could not live long."

Older women who could no longer perform heavy labor were sometimes placed in charge of the youngest slave children so that their mothers could return to the fields. Children usually began running errands and performing other light chores around age six. They went to work in the big house or the fields between the ages of eight and twelve. One historian has estimated that about half of all slave children were sold away from at least one of their parents before reaching adulthood.

Slave owners often tried to increase their wealth by forcing or encouraging their female slaves to have babies. Some masters promised freedom to slave women who gave birth to a certain number of babies. Former slave Jennie Hill recalled with bitterness that her master seemed to believe that slaves

bore their children as animals bear their young and that there was no heart-break when the children were torn from their parents or the mother taken from her brood to toil for a master in another state. . . . I would sit in my room with the little ones on my lap and the tears would roll down my cheeks as I would ponder the right and wrong of bringing them into the world. . . . They couldn't be educated and maybe they couldn't even live with their families. They would just be slaves.

THE SLAVE QUARTERS

At the end of their long workday, laborers on small farms might retire to a barn or other outbuilding. Slaves who lived on large plantations were housed in the slave quarters. (On both large and small farms, house servants often slept on the floor of the kitchen or in the doorway of their master's bedroom.) The families in the slave quarters lived in small brick, wood, or log cabins, which were grouped together out of sight of the big house. There might be one or two families in each small cabin. The chinks in the rough walls were often stuffed with moss, mud, or grass to keep out the cold and drafts. There was a fireplace at one end of the cabin for cooking the evening meal.

Brick slave cabins at the Hermitage Plantation in Savannah, Georgia. Nearly two hundred slaves lived and worked on this large rice plantation.

Masters distributed a supply of food to each family once a week. The slaves' diet consisted mainly of rice, cornmeal, and bacon or salt pork, plus sweet potatoes, molasses, and other foods when available. Many masters allowed their slaves to raise hens for eggs and tend small vegetable gardens. In addition, slaves often supplemented their diet with wild berries, fish, and animals such as raccoons or rabbits, which they trapped or hunted.

Plantation owners also provided their slaves with clothing or material to make clothes. Field hands typically received one to four changes of clothes a year. These included pants and shirts for the men, dresses for the women, and long shirts for the children. The clothes were made from homespun cloth woven by the slave women or from rough "Negro cloth," which northern textile mills manufactured especially for southern slaveholders. Fanny Kemble wrote that "the allowance of clothing . . . was given out at Christmas for the year, and consisted of one pair of coarse shoes, and enough coarse cloth to make a jacket and trowsers. . . . The women receive their allowance of the same kind of cloth which the men have. This they make into a frock; if they have any under garments they must procure [get] them for themselves."

The wretched living quarters, poor diet, and grueling workload took their toll on slaves' health. In Louisiana, where owners of sugar plantations worked their slaves especially hard, the life expectancy for a black female slave born in 1850 was thirty-four years; for a male, it was twenty-nine years. A large proportion of slaves also sickened and died in the swampy lowlands of South Carolina and Georgia. In many other areas, however, the death rate of slaves was only slightly higher than that of white southerners.

CONTROL AND PUNISHMENT

Despite the cruelties of the slave system, plantation owners insisted that slavery actually benefited blacks. In their view black people were inferior beings who were incapable of caring for themselves properly. If these "grown-up children" were not guided and protected by their white masters, they would fall into laziness, thievery, and drunkenness. George Fitzhugh, a white planter and lawyer from Virginia, asserted that "negro slavery" was "the most necessary of all human institutions. . . .

THE OVERSEER'S LASH

On large plantations slaveholders usually hired white overseers to supervise the slaves and deal out punishments. Wes Brady grew up in slavery on a cotton plantation in Texas, where the field hands worked under an overseer's watchful eye and ready lash.

The overseer was 'straddle his big horse at three o'clock in the mornin', roustin' the hands off to the field. He got them all lined up and then come back to the house for breakfas'. The rows was a mile long and no matter how much grass was in them, if you leaves one sprig on your row they beats you nearly to death. . . . The overseer give [the slaves] fifteen minutes to git dinner. He'd start cuffin' some of them over the head when it was time to stop eatin' and go back to work. He'd go to the house and eat his dinner and then he'd come back and look in all the buckets and if a piece of anything that was there when he left was et, he'd say you was losin' time and had to be whipped. He'd drive four stakes in the ground and tie a [slave] down and beat him till he's raw.

Above: This man, known only as Gordon, escaped from slavery in Mississippi to freedom in the North, carrying with him the scars from numerous whippings.

From inferiority, or rather peculiarity, of race, almost all negroes require masters."

Many slaveholders thought of their slaves as part of their extended family—although a very troublesome and inferior part. In their role as "father," they believed that they had a duty to look after "their people" and keep them in line. Owners interfered in nearly every aspect of their slaves' lives, including work, health, marriage, children, and leisure activities. They drew up detailed rules governing when the slaves should get up in the morning and go to bed at night, what they should eat, and when they were permitted to fish, hunt, work their own gardens, trade, ride a horse, visit a neighboring plantation, and marry. When a child was born, the mother's owner often insisted on naming the newborn, ignoring the name given by the parents.

Beginning in the mid-1700s, many southern slave owners also made efforts to introduce their slaves to Christianity. Charles C. Jones, a Georgia minister and slaveholder, argued that God had enslaved Africans so that their masters could lift them "from the pit of ignorance, moral pollution and death into which they have fallen." Slaveholders could not ignore their "divinely imposed" obligation to convert their slaves from their "state of absolute Heathenism," wrote Jones, "without forfeiting our humanity, . . . and our claim to the spirit of christianity itself." A master who was determined to "save" his slaves regularly read the Bible to his household, black and white. He might insist that slaves go to church on Sundays or give them the choice of attending church or working.

The real reason that slaveholders constantly intruded in the lives of their slaves was to control their human property, body and soul. Masters had one more tool for imposing their will: violence. A few owners never beat their slaves. However, most believed that the threat of physical punishment and an occasional "correction" were essential to maintaining order and discipline. Especially cruel masters inflicted constant punishments for small or imagined offenses. Lewis Clark, who worked in the big house on a plantation in Kentucky, recalled that there was hardly a week when he or one of his fellow slaves "did not receive some kind of beating or abuse" at the hands of their mistress. "It seemed as though she could not live nor sleep unless some poor back was smarting, some head beating with pain, or some eye filled with tears, around her."

Along with beatings, owners used other methods to punish their slaves. They might withhold food or privileges. They might humiliate a defiant male slave by forcing him to wear a dress and perform "women's work." Some owners locked disobedient slaves in stocks, cages, or private jails. Others made their "troublemakers," male and female, wear iron collars, arm and leg shackles, or a cruel device known as the "iron muzzle," which was clamped over the mouth to prevent eating, drinking, and speaking. The most dreaded punishment was sale. Slaveholders might try to control a rebellious slave by threatening to sell members of his or her family. At the same time, they defended the practice of breaking up slave families by claiming that blacks were incapable of forming the same deep and loving attachments as whites.

Chapter 5

QUIET RESISTANCE

IN 1831 JAMES HENRY HAMMOND ACQUIRED SILVER Bluff, a large estate in South Carolina. Hammond disapproved of the work habits of the 147 slaves on the plantation. He designed a new management system that would give him "absolute control" over every area of his workers' lives. The planter replaced the task system of labor, in which each worker performed a daily chore independently, with the gang system, in which slaves worked under the supervision of an overseer. He instructed his overseer to use small rewards and frequent punishments to encourage hard work and obedience. He also drew up detailed rules regarding what was expected and what was forbidden in areas such as marriage, child care, worship, and leisure activities. Slaves who broke the rules or neglected their work were to be punished with no more than "100 lashes in one

Slaves could be punished in any way an owner saw fit, and imprisoned for almost any reason.

day," administered "calmly and deliberately." The planter urged his overseer to use "fairness, justness and moderation in all things. . . . Inspire a negro with perfect confidence in you, learn him to look to you for support, and he is your slave."

Hammond's efforts to make his slave laborers dependent and obedient were not entirely successful. While the slaves at Silver Bluff lived and worked under strict supervision, they still managed to retain a measure of independence. They did so little work under the restrictive gang labor system that the planter was forced to return to task labor. They continued to practice forbidden activities in secret. In addition, between 1831 and 1835, fifty-three slaves ran away from the plantation. Lamenting his losses, Hammond wrote that he had "adopted every possible measure" to promote his slaves' health and happiness and that he was "one of the most unfortunate of men."

Abuse and mistreatment drove many slaves to despair and sometimes even to suicide.

STRUGGLES OVER LABOR

The majority of African Americans accepted the hopelessness of fighting a society that was determined to oppress them. Most slaves resigned themselves to spending their entire lives laboring without pay for white masters. At the same time, slaves rejected the *right* of those masters to enslave them. And, like the laborers on Silver Bluff plantation, they used a variety of methods to resist their oppressors, assert their humanity, and control at least a portion of their lives.

Slaves spent the greater part of each day working, so it is not surprising that much of their day-to-day resistance centered on the control of their labor. There were many ways for a seemingly obedient worker to reduce his work output and cut into his master's profits. Slaves pretended to be too sick to work or too stupid to understand simple orders. They broke or lost tools. They worked carelessly, damaging the growing crops or the harvest. Out of sight of the master or overseer, they slowed down or simply stopped working.

More active forms of resistance included theft and sabotage. Slaves stole whatever they could from their masters, reasoning that they were entitled to property that had been accumulated through their own labor. Food, tobacco, liquor, and various other items from the storehouse and big house ended up in the slave quarters. In some areas slaves set up elaborate trading networks to exchange stolen goods with their contacts on neighboring plantations. Slaves also struck out at their masters by damaging property (such as farm equipment, fences, and wagons) and even burning down barns and other plantation buildings.

Frustrated slaveholders often responded to slave resistance by offering rewards such as extra food or tobacco to hard workers. Like James Henry Hammond, some masters switched from gang labor to the task labor system. Slaves who had a specific task to complete each day had a reason to work quickly. When they finished their task, they were free to work for themselves. In their free time, slaves might hunt, fish, work in their gardens, or practice crafts such as weaving, basket making, wood carving, or carpentry.

Some masters allowed their slaves to earn money by selling their handcrafted goods. Some hired out their most skilled workers to neighboring planters. Slaves who were hired out had to turn over all or part of their wages to their owner. This practice brought benefits not only to the planter but also to the worker. Through their special knowledge and skills, slaves enjoyed a small measure of independence and sometimes earned a small income. They also took pride in disproving white slaveholders' claims that blacks were naturally lazy and inferior.

THE FLIGHT TO FREEDOM

Another common act of defiance was running away. Every year thousands of slaves escaped from southern plantations. Most fugitives fled to avoid work or punishment or to spend time with a loved one on a neighboring plantation. After a few days

A fugitive slave hides from pursuers. If he is caught and returned to his master, he will be severely punished for running away.

or weeks, these "short-term" runaways usually returned, tired and hungry, or were discovered hiding out in the woods or swamps within a few miles of their homes.

Some fugitives stayed away for longer periods. After hitting her mistress, a young house servant on a Georgia plantation took refuge inside a cave in a nearby swamp. Over time her husband, who was a slave on the same plantation, made a cozy home inside the cave. He put in a stove and constructed a ceiling, bed, and tables from pine logs. He brought food, which was scraped together by the other slaves on the plantation. The woman lived in the cave for seven years, bearing three children there. Finally, the Civil War brought freedom to her and her family.

Many other slaves fled their masters' homes in order to escape bondage completely. Most of the fugitives who made their way to the northern free states were young men from the upper South, especially from Maryland, Virginia, Kentucky, and Missouri. Women were less likely to run to freedom. Most young slave women had babies and small children, and it was very hard to make the journey north with a family.

Even on their own, fugitives who were headed north faced a long and difficult journey. Few slaves could read or write. Their knowledge of geography was usually limited to the vague idea that freedom lay in the direction of the North Star. Most run-aways traveled on foot, crossing through miles of unfamiliar country under the cover of darkness. Others made it to freedom by stealing horses, stowing away on boats, or even packing themselves in boxes to be shipped north. Many received help from the abolitionist network known as the Underground Rail-road. (To learn more about the Underground Railroad, see volume 4 in this series, *The Civil War.*)

Escaped slaves sometimes forged or borrowed passes or the identification papers of free blacks. Men might disguise themselves as women. Light-skinned blacks might pass as white. Ellen Craft, a fair-skinned slave from Georgia, escaped with her husband, William, by pretending to be his white master.

Slaveholders did everything in their power to recover fugitives. Patrols made up of planters and hired guns watched the roads, stopping black travelers to check their passes. Owners advertised in the newspapers, describing their runaway slaves and offering rewards for the fugitives' recovery. Some masters hired "Negro hunters," who pursued runaways with packs of dogs that were trained to track and attack on command. Fugitives who were recaptured faced harsh punishments. Many were brutally whipped or beaten. Some were mutilated, shot, or hanged.

$100 REWARD

WILL be given for the apprehension and delivery of my Servant Girl HARRIET. She is a light mulatto, 21 years of age, about 5 feet 4 inches high, of a thick and corpulent habit, having on her head a thick covering of black hair that curls naturally, but which can be easily combed straight. She speaks easily and fluently, and has an agreeable carriage and address. Being a good seamstress, she has been accustomed to dress well, has a variety of very fine clothes, made in the prevailing fashion, and will probably appear, if abroad, tricked out in gay and fashionable finery. As this girl absconded from the plantation of my son without any known cause or provocation, it is probable she designs to transport herself to the North.

The above reward, with all reasonable charges, will be given for apprehending her, or securing her in any prison or jail within the U. States.

All persons are hereby forewarned against harboring or entertaining her, or being in any way instrumental in her escape, under the most rigorous penalties of the law.
JAMES NORCOM.
Edenton, N. C. June 30

A newspaper advertisement seeks the capture of an escaped slave known as Harriet Jacobs.

In spite of all the difficulties and dangers, slaves continued to seek freedom. Many fugitives made it to the North on their second or third tries. Henry Bibb, who was born a slave on a Kentucky plantation, fled to Ohio but was recaptured when he returned for his family. After several more escape attempts,

Bibb made it to Canada, where he became a leader of the abolitionist cause. Bibb later wrote that in slavery, he "learned the art of running away to perfection. . . . I made a regular business of it, and never gave it up, until I had broken the bands of slavery, and landed myself safely in Canada, where I was regarded as a man, and not as a thing."

AFRICAN-AMERICAN CULTURE

Slaves also asserted their humanity and independence by building a community all their own. The African-American community began with the family. Masters disrupted slave families in many ways. They forced strangers to marry in order to produce children, took married women as their mistresses, and broke up families through sale. Despite all these obstacles, enslaved men and women continued to fall in love, marry, and maintain strong emotional ties, which often endured long after separation.

A portrait of Henry Bibb from *Narrative of the Life and Adventures of Henry Bibb, an American Slave, Written by Himself*. Published in 1849, Bibb's book was one of the most influential slave narratives.

Families used names to strengthen their family ties. While some owners insisted on naming their newborn slaves, usually giving them first names only, parents gave their children "titles," or last names. Those titles sometimes reached all the way back to Africa. More often they reflected a child's relation to its father, helping slaves keep track of their families through the generations. Former slave Robert Smalls recalled that

"A GREATER SIN"

Slaveholders who were convinced that their "people" needed and appreciated their "protection" were outraged when a slave escaped to freedom. After Jarmain Wesley Loguen escaped from slavery in Tennessee, his former master tracked him down to New York but was unable to recapture him. Loguen later received a letter from his former mistress, accusing him of theft and ingratitude. Here is part of his reply:

You say "You know we raised you as we did our own children." Woman, did you raise your own children for the market? Did you raise them for the whipping post? Did you raise them to be driven off, bound to a coffle in chains? Where are my poor bleeding brothers and sisters? Can you tell? Who was it that sent them off into sugar and cotton fields, to be kicked and cuffed, and whipped, and to groan and die; and where no kin can hear their groans. . . ? You say I am a thief, because I took the old mare along with me. Have you got to learn that I had a better right to the old mare, as you call her, than [Master] has to me? Is it a greater sin for me to steal his horse, than it was for him to rob my mother's cradle, and steal me?

slaves used their titles only "among themselves. . . . [B]efore their masters they do not speak of their titles at all."

Many slaves also forged ties with a large extended family that might include both distant relatives and friends. Members of this close-knit slave community helped one another by caring for the young and aged. They tried to protect one another from the slaveholders' power. House servants might bring food to a runaway hiding out in a nearby forest or swamp. Field hands might add cotton to the basket of a coworker who was unable to pick her day's quota.

Most interactions between members of the slave community took place in the slave quarters. There black men, women, and children spent their few free hours relaxing together, out of sight of masters and overseers. They talked, sang, danced, ate, drank, and played games. Over time they created a unique African-American culture that blended their African roots with southern white culture. They told traditional stories adapted from African languages to English, often featuring ghosts, spirits, and small animals who outwitted their stronger but less clever rivals. They prepared herbal remedies that were sometimes more effective than the white doctors' medicines. They practiced magic, using charms and potions to win a lover's heart or make an owner more merciful.

Slaves played music on African instruments such as drums and banjos. They sang field chants and work songs with traditional musical harmonies and rhythms, which gradually evolved into a fresh new musical form. One feature of African-American music was its use of call-and-response, in which a leader sang a musical phrase and the chorus sang a reply.

Vinnie Brunson, who was born into slavery in Texas, recalled that music was a part of everyday life on the plantation.

> The [slave] used to sing to nearly everything he did. . . . If he was happy, it made him happy, if he was sad it made him feel better. . . . The timber [man] he sings as he cuts the logs and keeps the time with his axe. The women sing as they bend over the washtub, the cotton chopper sing as he chops the cotton. The mother sing as she rocks her baby to sleep. . . . It was the [slaves'] mos' joy, and his mos' comfort.

Music was also an important part of worship. Slaves developed their own unique form of Christianity, which combined African and white Christian practices. This new faith gave a

This 1894 painting by African-American artist Henry Ossawa Tanner expresses the importance of religion in many black families both during and after slavery.

special meaning to traditional Christian beliefs, emphasizing the worshipper's personal relationship with God and the promise of deliverance from oppression. Religion, in fact, provided a refuge for many enslaved African Americans, and its importance in helping them resist tyranny cannot be overstated. Communities of faith grew and flourished, helping people find support in one another. Prayer meetings were often held in secret, because masters feared the power of religion and tried to prevent the slaves from worshipping without white supervision. Black preachers, too, often took great risks sneaking out of their plantations to spread the word of God.

African-American religious services reflected the new musical form. Lively call-and-response spirituals blended African rhythms with the words of European hymns. Some white observers were shocked by the emotional fervor of African-American religion. One minister described a black service as "one loud monotonous strain, interrupted by . . . groans and screams and clapping of hands." For their part, slaves often found white religious services dull and stuffy. "You see," explained one worshipper, "[re]ligion needs a little motion—specially if you gwine feel the spirit."

Chapter 6

OPEN REBELLION

WHILE AFRICAN AMERICANS MOST OFTEN RESISTED slavery through peaceful means, their anger over their inhumane treatment sometimes erupted in violence. Most acts of violent rebellion were individual and unplanned. A slave who had been abused again and again might suddenly reach the boiling point and strike back at his or her master. Organized rebellions involving a number of people were far less common. However, there were enough slave rebellions and rumors of rebellions to keep slaveholders in a constant state of anxiety. Fanny Kemble, who visited Charleston, South Carolina, in 1838, observed armed guards patrolling the streets for black "troublemakers." "No doubt these daily and nightly precautions are but trifling drawbacks upon the manifold [many] blessings of slavery," she wrote, "still, I should prefer going to

A slave turns on the overseer who was about to whip him.

sleep without the apprehension of my servants' cutting my throat in my bed."

Adding to the slaveholders' anxiety was the difficulty of telling which slaves were harmless and which were potential rebels. To protect themselves from suspicion and punishment, nearly all slaves wore a "mask of obedience." No matter how angry they might feel, they pretended to be meek, loyal, and contented. Slaveholders who claimed that slavery was a positive institution were eager to accept this pretense. However, they could never be entirely sure what lay beneath their servants' masks. "So deceitful is the Negro," complained one southern planter, "that as far as my own experience extends I could never in a single instance decipher his character."

"Resolved to Fight"

Mary Armstrong of Missouri was about ten years old when she took revenge on a former mistress who had brutally beaten her nine-month-old sister. The young slave girl picked up "a rock about as big as half your fist and hits her right in the eye and busted the eyeball, and tells her that's for whippin' my baby sister to death. You could hear her holler for five miles."

William Lee of Virginia got tired of the constant beatings he received from his mistress. This cruel woman used to hold his head between her legs as she whacked his back. One day Lee grabbed her legs and "bodily carried ole missus out an' thro' her on de ground jes' as hard as I could."

Abram, who was a slave in Alabama during the Civil War, became enraged when an overseer whipped him for claiming that he was too sick to work. Abram grabbed the whip, then knocked a gun out of the overseer's hand. He threw the man to the ground and bit off part of his ear as they struggled.

Frederick Douglass was a defiant young slave in Maryland when his master sent him to a "slave breaker" named Edward Covey. Douglass later recalled that Covey worked him night and day, whipping him mercilessly, until he was "broken in body, soul, and spirit." One day, when Covey seized him for yet another beating, Douglass "resolved to fight." For nearly two hours, the men boxed and wrestled. Finally, the worn-out slave breaker gave up, "puffing and blowing at a great rate, saying that if I had not resisted, he would not have whipped me half so much. The truth was, that he had not whipped me at all."

Masters and overseers rarely talked about incidents such as these. It was too embarrassing for a slaveholder to admit that he had been challenged or overpowered by an "inferior" who was supposedly under his complete control. Nevertheless, the diaries of planters, interviews with former slaves, and other records show that such confrontations were surprisingly common.

After using force against their masters, most slaves ran away to avoid punishment. Those who were caught faced severe penalties. Slaves could be executed for wounding or killing a white person, even if they had acted in self-defense. An Alabama court convicted Abram of "mayhem" for biting off the overseer's ear and sentenced him to death. Soon after the end of the Civil War, however, Abram's case was appealed to the Alabama Supreme Court, which ruled that both "the bound and the free" had the right to inflict a wound when their lives were threatened.

In some cases, acts of rebellion actually improved a slave's lot. After fighting Edward Covey, Frederick Douglass was never beaten again. Years later, Douglass realized that Covey had avoided further confrontations because he did not want to ruin his reputation as "a first-rate overseer and Negro-breaker." The former slave concluded that

> he is whipped oftenest, who is whipped easiest;
> that slave who has the courage to stand up for him-
> self against the overseer, although he may have
> many hard stripes at the first, becomes, in the end,
> a freeman, even though he sustain the formal rela-
> tion of a slave.

Conspiracies and Rebellions

Individual acts of rebellion rarely grew into mass uprisings. Due to a number of factors, slaves had little chance of planning and carrying out a widespread revolt. Whites greatly outnumbered blacks in most of the South. The majority of slaves lived on scattered farms and plantations, where they were closely watched by armed overseers and masters. Laws and practices such as the slave patrols sharply restricted the movements and contacts of both slaves and free blacks. In addition, slaves who managed to meet and plan an uprising faced the constant threat of betrayal. Even fellow slaves might betray a conspiracy out of loyalty to a white master or in hopes of earning a reward.

Despite all these factors, some groups of slaves did plan rebellions, dating back to the earliest days of colonial America. The first known slave conspiracy took place in Gloucester County, Virginia, in 1663. A small group of African slaves and white indentured servants plotted to overthrow their masters and escape to freedom. The plot was foiled, however, when one of the servants betrayed his fellow conspirators to the authorities.

In April 1712 a more deadly conspiracy was put into action in New York City. A group of African slaves set fire to a slaveholder's house. According to a local minister, "the fire alarmed the town, who from all parts ran to it; the conspirators planted themselves in several streets and lanes leading to the fire, and shot or stabbed the people as they were running to it." By the time the militia put down the revolt, the rebels "had killed about 8 and wounded 12 more."

The Stono Rebellion of 1739 took the lives of about forty slaves and twenty slaveholders. Slaves in South Carolina had learned that the Spanish colony of Florida was granting freedom to captives who escaped from the British colonies. Under the leadership of a former African soldier named Jemmy, about twenty slaves in Stono, outside Charleston, armed themselves and headed for Florida. As they marched through the countryside,

MAROON COMMUNITIES

After rebelling against their masters, some runaway slaves took refuge with maroon communities. These were organized groups of fugitives who lived in remote, sparsely settled areas of the South. Most maroons survived by raiding farms and stealing food, clothing, livestock, and other items. They also might trade with free blacks and friendly whites and Indians.

Maroon communities usually traveled from place to place. Sometimes, though, they formed permanent settlements. The largest maroon community lived in the heart of the Great Dismal Swamp, along the border between Virginia and North Carolina. One eighteenth-century visitor described the Great Dismal Swamp as "a filthy bog in a vast body of nastiness." About two thousand fugitives chose to live and raise their families in this harsh wilderness rather than submit to slavery.

Fugitive slaves take shelter in the Great Dismal Swamp.

they plundered and burned plantations, killing slaveholders known for their cruelty but sparing those who had treated their slaves well. Jemmy's army swelled to more than a hundred rebels before it was stopped by a group of armed planters.

NINETEENTH-CENTURY UPRISINGS

In the early nineteenth century, slaves fought back against their oppressors in several large conspiracies and uprisings. The first attempted rebellion took place in the summer of 1800. Gabriel Prosser, an enslaved blacksmith in Richmond, Virginia, devised a plan that he hoped would frighten whites into granting slaves their freedom. Prosser raised a secret army of several thousand rebels and stored away a supply of homemade weapons. He planned to seize weapons and government buildings in Richmond and overcome the city's white residents. On the night of the attack, however, a violent storm washed out the roads and bridges leading to the city, preventing the rebels from assembling. Two slaves betrayed the plot, and about thirty rebels, including Prosser, were executed.

In January 1811 the largest slave revolt in U.S. history terrified whites in Louisiana. Between five hundred and six hundred slaves formed into military companies and marched on New Orleans. As they pushed forward, the rebels burned plantations, picked up weapons, and gathered new recruits. State and local militias were quickly called out to suppress the rebellion. They mowed down every black person in sight, killing dozens of slaves.

In 1822 Denmark Vesey, a free black man living in Charleston, South Carolina, decided to free the city's slaves from their "abominable life." Vesey developed an elaborate

plot in which his slave army would burn the city and escape on ships seized in the harbor. Before he could put his plan into action, his conspiracy was betrayed to the authorities. More than one hundred black men and women were arrested, and thirty-five were hanged.

Nat Turner and some of his followers plan their rebellion.

Perhaps the most famous slave uprising was Nat Turner's Rebellion. Turner was a slave in Southampton County, Virginia, who believed that he was a prophet who had been born "for some great purpose." In August 1831 he led about seventy followers armed with guns, swords, and axes on a campaign to spread terror and devastation among white slave owners. Turner's men moved from plantation to plantation, killing nearly sixty white men, women, and children. They were finally overcome by a group of armed slaveholders and militiamen.

Following the defeat of Turner's forces, whites throughout the region went on their own rampage. Hundreds of slaves and free blacks who had played no part in the uprising were attacked and killed. Ten weeks after the start of his rebellion, Turner was captured and hanged. That put an end to the violence. However, Nat Turner and other slave rebels would live on in the nightmares of white southerners. They would also bring hope to African Americans, who saw them as a symbol of the slaves' determination to break their chains and avenge themselves on the slaveholders.

THE PRICE OF REBELLION

Slaveholders responded to slave rebellions with harsh punishments. Slaves who were suspected of involvement in conspiracies were often tortured and executed. Several of the slaves involved in the 1663 conspiracy in Gloucester County, Virginia, were beheaded. More than twenty blacks who were accused of taking part in the 1712 New York rebellion were starved to death, broken on the torturer's rack, or burned alive. After the 1811 uprising in Louisiana, the authorities displayed the heads of executed slaves on poles along the Mississippi River, to discourage other would-be rebels.

Slave rebellions also resulted in strict new controls on African Americans. For example, South Carolina responded to the Stono Rebellion by passing the Negro Act of 1740. Among its many restrictions, the law made it illegal for slaves to raise their own food, earn money, assemble in groups, learn to read or write, or testify in court. It also declared that any slave who conspired to run away or rebel against his or her master should be executed. Similar slave codes were enacted throughout the South right up to the Civil War, defending fearful whites from their nation's most defenseless citizens.

With all its abuses and indignities, slavery never crushed the spirits of African Americans. Through quiet resistance and open rebellion, they continued to fight back and proclaim their humanity. In time the struggles between the defenders and opponents of slavery would lead to the bloodiest war in U.S. history, and to a new birth of freedom.

Glossary

abolitionists People who favored abolishing, or putting an end to, slavery.

domestic slave trade The trading of slaves within and among the American colonies or states.

fugitive A person who flees or tries to escape.

gang system A system of labor in which a group of workers performs a job under close supervision.

heathenism Not believing in the God of the Jews, Christians, or Muslims.

imperceptible Very slight or gradual; hardly noticeable.

indigo A plant used to make a deep blue dye for textiles and cosmetics.

lacerated Cut or torn from injury.

lower South The southern slaveholding states of Alabama, Arkansas, Florida, Georgia, Louisiana, Mississippi, South Carolina, and Texas; also called the "deep South."

maroon A member of an organized community of fugitive slaves who lived in sparsely settled areas of Alabama, the Carolinas, Florida, Georgia, Louisiana, Mississippi, and Virginia. The term *maroon* came from the Spanish word *cimarrón*, meaning "wild" or "unruly."

mayhem The intentional and unlawful mutilation of another person.

militiamen Members of the citizen armies of the thirteen original American colonies.

Quakers Members of the Society of Friends, a Christian sect founded in England. Many Quakers came to New Jersey and Pennsylvania in the late 1600s.

sabotage The deliberate destruction of property in order to hinder an enemy.

slave breaker An overseer who specialized in "breaking" slaves by over-working and abusing them until they were too exhausted to rebel.

task system A system of labor in which each worker is assigned a particular daily chore to complete at his or her own pace.

transatlantic slave trade The capture of African men, women, and children and the transporting of those captives into slavery in the Americas.

upper South The southern slaveholding states of Delaware, Kentucky, Maryland, Missouri, North Carolina, Tennessee, and Virginia, plus Washington, DC.

To Find Out More

BOOKS

Altman, Linda Jacobs. *Slavery and Abolition in American History*. Berkeley Heights, NJ: Enslow Publishers, 1999.

Budd, Elizabeth S. *American Voices from the Time of Slavery*. New York: Benchmark Books, 2007.

Dudley, William, ed. *American Slavery*. San Diego: Greenhaven Press, 2000.

Greene, Meg. *Slave Young, Slave Long: The American Slave Experience*. Minneapolis: Lerner Publications, 1999.

Landau, Elaine. *Slave Narratives: The Journey to Freedom*. New York: Franklin Watts, 2001.

Schomp, Virginia. *Letters from the Battlefront: The Revolutionary War*. New York: Benchmark Books, 2004.

Tapper, Suzanne Cloud. *Voices from Slavery's Past: Yearning to Be Heard*. Berkeley Heights, NJ: Enslow Publishers, 2004.

WEB SITES

The African American: A Journey from Slavery to Freedom. Professor Melvin R. Sylvester. B. Davis Schwartz Memorial Library, C. W. Post Campus, Long Island University, 1998.
http://www.liu.edu/cwis/cwp/library/aaslavry.htm

Africans in America: The Terrible Transformation. WGBH Interactive and PBS Online. Copyright © 1998, 1999 WGBH Educational Foundation.
http://www.pbs.org/wgbh/aia/part1/title.html

Born in Slavery: Slave Narratives from the Federal Writers' Project, 1936-1938. Library of Congress, 2001.
http://memory.loc.gov/ammem/snhtml/snhome.html

Digital History: African-American Voices. S. Mintz. Copyright © 2005 Digital History.
http://www.digitalhistory.uh.edu/black_voices/black_voices.cfm

Selected Bibliography

Berlin, Ira. *Generations of Captivity: A History of African-American Slaves*. Cambridge, MA: Harvard University Press, 2003.

Berlin, Ira, Marc Favreau, and Steven F. Miller, eds. *Remembering Slavery: African Americans Talk about Their Personal Experiences of Slavery and Emancipation*. New York: New Press, 1998.

Franklin, John Hope, and Alfred A. Moss Jr. *From Slavery to Freedom: A History of African Americans.* New York: Alfred A. Knopf, 2004.

Franklin, John Hope, and Loren Schweninger. *Runaway Slaves: Rebels on the Plantations.* New York: Oxford University Press, 1999.

Halpern, Rick, and Enrico Dal Lago, eds. *Slavery and Emancipation.* Malden, MA: Blackwell Publishing, 2002.

Horton, James Oliver, and Lois E. Horton. *Slavery and the Making of America.* New York: Oxford University Press, 2005.

Johnson, Charles, and Patricia Smith. *Africans in America: America's Journey through Slavery.* New York: Harcourt Brace, 1998.

Kolchin, Peter. *American Slavery, 1619-1877.* New York: Hill and Wang, 2003.

Schneider, Dorothy, and Carl J. Schneider. *Slavery in America: From Colonial Times to the Civil War.* New York: Facts on File, 2001.

Schwartz, Marie Jenkins. *Born in Bondage: Growing Up Enslaved in the Antebellum South.* Cambridge, MA: Harvard University Press, 2000.

Wood, Peter H. *Strange New Land: Africans in Colonial America.* New York: Oxford University Press, 2003.

Index

Page numbers for illustrations are in boldface

abolition
  abolition movement, 17, 19, 22, 25
  abolitionists, 16–17, **17**, 29, 37, 51
Act to Prohibit the Importation of Slaves, 29
Adams, Abigail and John, 16, **16**
American Colonization Society, 34
Attucks, Crispus, 14–15, **14**

Ball, Charles, 30–31
Bibb, Henry, 52–53, **53**
Boston Massacre, **14**, 15
Brady, Wes, 43
Bunker Hill, Battle of, 17, 18, **18**

Christianity, 44, 56–57
Civil War, 27, 29, 51, 60, 61, 66
colonization movement, 34, **34**
Constitutional Convention, 23, 25

Continental army, 18, 20
cotton plantations, **22**, 26–27, **26**, 28, **28**, 29
Covey, Edward, 61–62
Craft, Ellen, 52
Cuffee, Paul, 34, **34**

Declaration of Independence, 17–18
domestic slave trade, 28–31, **30**
Douglass, Frederick, 37, 61–62
Dutch West India Company, 9, 10

Finley, Robert, 34
First Continental Congress, 13–14
Fitzhugh, George, 42, 44
Florida, slavery in, 6, 8, 28
free blacks, 1, 7, 10, 11, 31–33, **32**, 35
Fugitive Slave Act, 32–33

gang labor system, 47–48, 49
Georgia, slavery in, 6, 28, 29, **41**, 42

Grosvenor, Thomas, **18**

Hammond, James Henry, 47–48, 49
Henry, Patrick, **12**, 14

indentured servants, 2, 3–4, 7, 8, 62
indigo plantations, 6, 8, 26

Jay, John, 16
Jefferson, Thomas, 18, 19, 27, 29
Johnson, Anthony and Mary, 1–2, 5, 11

Kemble, Fanny, 39, 42, 59–60

labor
    backbreaking labor, 38–39, **38**
    labor struggles and slave resistance,
        48–50
Lafayette, James Armistead, **16**
laws
    concerning free blacks, 32–33
    Negro Act of 1740, 66
    slave codes, 4–5, 6, 7
Lexington and Concord, Battles of,
    17, 18
Loguen, Jarmain Wesley, 54
Louisiana Purchase, 27–28

maroon communities, 63, **63**
Maryland, slavery in, 2–5, 29, 31
Middle Colonies, slavery in, 7, 9–11, **9**, **10**
Murray, John (Earl of Dunmore), 20
music, African-American, 55–56

New England Colonies, slavery in,
    8–9, 10–11, **21**

plantation life, **36**, 37–45, **38**, **40**, **41**, **43**
Prosser, Gabriel, 64
punishment, control and, **4**, 11, 42–45,
    43, **46**, 47–48, **48**, 60

Quakers, 16–17, **17**

Revolutionary War, **12**, 13–14, 25, 28, 33
    choosing sides, 18, **18**, 20
    conflicts and contradictions, 15–17,
        16, **17**
    constitutional compromises, 21–23,
        21, **22**
    Declaration of Independence, 17–18
    "Liberty! Liberty!," 14–15, **14**
rice plantations, 5, 6, **6**, 8, 26, **41**
runaway slaves (fugitives), 20, 32–33,
    50–53, **50**, **52**, 61, 63, **63**
Rush, Benjamin, 23

Salem, Peter, 17, 18, **18**
Second Continental Congress, 17–18
slave auctions, **x**, **24**, 32
slave codes, 4–5, 6, 7
slave quarters, 41–42, **41**
slave rebellions and uprisings, 18, **58**,
    59–66, **63**, **65**
slavery in colonial America, **x**, 1–11,
    3, **4**, **6**, **8**, **10**
Smalls, Robert, 53, 55
South Carolina, slavery in, 5–6, **26**,
    28, 29, 42, 59, 63–64, 65, 66
Stono Rebellion, 63–64, 66

tobacco, 1, 3, **3**, 5, 26
transatlantic slave trade, 9, 22, 28–29
Turner, Nat, 65–66, **65**

Underground Railroad, 51

Vesey, Denmark, 64–65
Virginia, slavery in, 1–5, **3**, **4**, 29, 30
    Thomas Jefferson, 18, 19, 27, 29

Washington, George, 18, 21, 25
Whitney, Eli, 26–27
women and children, enslaved, 20,
    39–40, **40**, 51